F IN EXAMS POP QUIZ

All New Awesomely Wrong Test Answers

Richard Benson

CHRONICLE BOOKS

SAN FRANCISCO

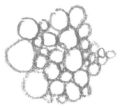

First published in the United States in 2015 by Chronicle Books LLC.

The contents of this book were published in the United Kingdom in 2013 and 2014 by Summersdale Publishers Ltd. under the titles *F in School* and *F in Spelling*. Copyright © 2013 and 2014 by Summersdale Publishers Ltd. All rights reserved. No part of this book may be reproduced in any from without permission from the publisher.

Library of Congress Cataloging-in-Publication Data available.

ISBN 978-1-4521-4403-0

Manufactured in China

MIX
Paper from
responsible sources
FSC® C008047
FSC
www.fsc.org

Designed by Liam Flanagan

10 9 8 7 6 5 4 3 2 1

Chronicle Books LLC
680 Second Street
San Francisco, California 94107
www.chroniclebooks.com

Contents

Introduction

Will some students ever learn from their mistakes? I, for one, certainly hope not.

Without that lurching, freefall feeling when you don't know the answer to the quiz question staring up from the page—we've all been there at one time or another—these students wouldn't have found the inspiration to look deep within themselves to find . . . not the answer, but something better instead.

Of course a little studying would reveal that the most powerful light source known to man isn't "lightsabers," nor do we salt the roads when it snows "to make them taste better," and that the Treaty of Versailles wasn't signed by "King Louis the Something," but where's the fun in that?

Thankfully, here for us all to enjoy is a fresh batch of A+ wit misapplied to F- quiz scores.

Biology and Chemistry

Subject: ....

Name a living organism that contains chlorophyll.

THE INCREDIBLE HULK

What part of the body is affected by glandular fever?

The glandular.

Describe the role of antibodies.

They are married to
     uncle bodies.

What is the purpose of red blood cells?

To keep blood the right color.

Name the five senses.

1. Nonsense
2. Suspense
3. Incense
4. Common sense
5. Seeing Ghosts

Explain the meaning of the term myopic.

It's when someone makes a biopic, but it's about themselves.

What is the primary function of alveoli?

a dip for potato chips

Explain the benefits of proteins.

people who are pro-teens make
sure young people's opinions are
taken seriously.

How does your humerus differ from your fibula?

One's funny and the other lies a lot.

Give examples of anaerobic activity.

ZUMBA is an aerobic activity

In order to survive, plants must sometimes compete with other plants. Name something that plants compete for.

Jumping-bean competitions.

TASTE!

HOW DID IT

Explain how plants compete.

Most plants play fair, but Venus flytraps BITE.

What effects can low blood sugar have on a person?

Sweet feet, leading to bees in your shoes

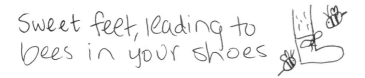

What effects can high blood sugar have on a person?

Sweet head, leading to bees in your hair

Explain when monkeys and apes began to evolve, and explain how.

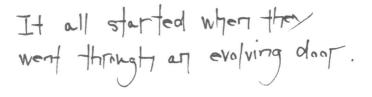

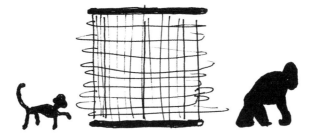

What do we call the chemical reaction between a fuel and an oxidant when heated?

FIRE! I love fire.

What is the process in which sugars convert to gases, acids and/or alcohol?

 Puberty

Give two examples of hydrocarbons.

pepsi + coke

What is the carbon cycle?

An expensive kind of bike.

What is the chemical formula for water?

Faucet + turn = water

What three elements need to be present to start a fire?

1. STICKS
2. A MATCH
3. SOMETHING TO LIGHT THE MATCH ON.

What are nanoparticles?

The tiny pieces that grannies are made of.

In comparison with large hydrocarbons, how would you describe small hydrocarbons?

they are smaller

Why is methane a gas at 20 degrees Celsius?

BECAUSE THAT'S
THE TEMPERATURE
OF A FART

Why is Mars red?

Because it's embarrassed
by Uranus

Why is chlorine added to tap water?

To make it taste less of pee.

What is the purpose of amylase?

It lets people
named Amy relax

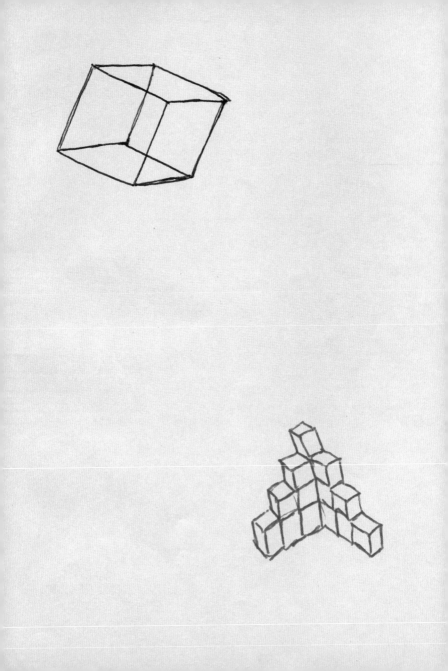

Subject: *Math*

= 8,008

How do you calculate the volume of a prism?

Count all the prisoners. The more prisoners, the louder it will be.

Two friends share $18 at a ratio of 6:3. How much do they each receive?

An unfair amount, if one friend is getting more than the other.

Draw a trapezium.

Write the number 32545346 in words.

Three two five four
five three four six

The probability that Steve oversleeps is three times the probability that he does not. Work out the probability that he does oversleep.

Depends — is
is it Monday?

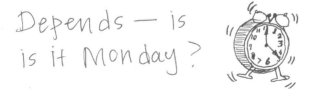

Draw a polygon.

Jane works in a café. She wants to work out if more men than women eat cake. Design an observation sheet for her.

Can you name three types of angle?

Charlie's Angles:
Sabrina, Jill,
and Kelly

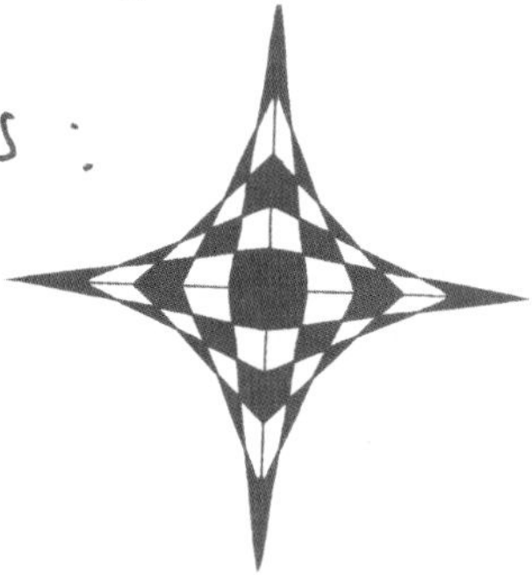

Define a triangle.

THE MOST BORING INSTRUMENT
IN THE ORCHESTRA

What is the name of a six-sided polygon?

SIXAgon

Define a pentagram.

Something you use to summon the Devil

How do we know this is a right angle?

Because a left angle
looks like this

In a supermarket one can of tuna costs 79 cents.
How many cans could you buy for $3.85?

Well, do they have a two for
one deal going on?

Subject: *Physics*

What are fossil fuels?

What you need to power a dinosaur

Where and how are fossil fuels extracted?

Mostly by grinding up old dinosaurs

What gas is produced when fossil fuels are burned?

smoke

How is burning fossil fuels harmful to the atmosphere?

the smoke makes you cough

What type of electricity production harnesses the power of the sea?

turtle power

Give ways that a homeowner can generate and store their own electricity.

Invest in a human hamster wheel.

Explain ways that a household energy bill can be reduced.

Tear it into small pieces

What determines the pitch of a sound?

How angry the person making it is

Why do the windows steam up on the inside of a car on a wet day?

Because it's too rainy to kiss outside, so people have to do it in their cars.

What does "thinking distance" mean in terms of a vehicle stopping?

It's the distance you drive when you think of something you left at home & you have to stop and go back for it.

What affects braking distance?

It depends on when you last stopped for a brake.

What does the Law of Gravity refer to?

I don't know, but it sounds very serious.

What is a hybrid car?

Chitty Chitty Bang Bang

What is a thermal conductor?

someone who leads
the orchestra in
long johns.

What are lasers used for?

So sharks can shoot beams
from their heads

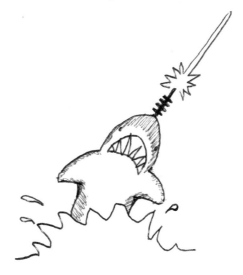

How is nuclear fission used to generate electricity?

By getting all the nuclear
fish to swim in the same direction

Explain how a transformer works.

IT'S A TRUCK, THEN IT'S A ROBOT.

An astronomer uses a telescope to observe the movement of stars and planets. Give one advantage of having a telescope at the top of a high mountain rather than the bottom.

The mountain doesn't get in the way.

Subject: .... *English* ....

What is one of the key themes running through
The Diary of Anne Frank?

Anne Frank's Dairy had lots of cows
running through it.

Lord of the Flies is often described as "terrifying."
Describe an incident in the book which is
terrifying.

THE BIT WHERE ALL THE FLIES COME
OUT AT ONCE IS QUITE SCARY, BUT
IT'S HARDLY THE EVIL DEAD.

Many believe that Piggy suffers the most in *Lord of the Flies*. Do you agree? Give reasons.

Yes. It's because they make him into an escape goat, because he's named after a farm animal.

What advice would you give an actor playing Piggy?

Remember that Kermit loves you.

Write about a time when either pride or prejudice is important in the novel.

Right at the start on the title page.

What are your first impressions of Mr Darcy in *Pride and Prejudice*?

He has very good manors.

Write about the character that has the greatest effect on Scrooge in *A Christmas Carol*.

The Ghost of Christmas Present, because he reminds Scrooge to buy Christmas presents.

Write about the importance of animals in *Of Mice and Men*.

The mice are very important — without them you'd only have the men

Explain the meaning of the word "dystopia."

i had dystopia once after eating a bad burger.

Explain what a colon is. Demonstrate how it should be applied in a sentence.

It's a kind of perfume for men. You spray it on your neck to make yourself smell nice.

What does Antonym mean?

I don't know what he means, but I think you've spelled his name wrong.

Write the longest sentence you can, using appropriate punctuation.

50 years to life.

Use the word "fascinate" in a sentence without changing the tense.

We bought my dad a shirt for his birthday. It had ten buttons, but because of his belly, he was only able to fascinate nine.

Define and give an example of an oxymoron.

An idiot who looks like a bull—
my uncle Manny.

A competition has been launched to find young people to join an expedition to the South Pole. Write a brief letter to persuade the organizers that you would be a great asset to the team.

My mom says I have a warm personality, so I wouldn't get cold. I also like penguins.

Subject: *Religious Studies* ....

— UP HERE!

What is an icon?

LADY GAGA

What is fasting?

Not HALF AS EXCITING
   AS   SLOWING.

What do you understand by the following commandment: "Thou shalt not commit adultery"?

You shouldn't pretend to be an adult if you're not one.

Is life better or worse if people observe the Ten Commandments? Explain your answer.

Anyone can observe them, but life is better if people actually do them too.

What do you understand by the term "afterlife"?

it's a computer game that some people get addicted to.

Can God's existence be proven? Give an example.

I heard someone say "Thank God it's Friday!" last Friday.

How is a rosary used?

It goes well with lamb
or in Italian food

Give the names of two symbols found in a synagogue.

Usually, you shouldn't play
The symbols in a synagogue

What happened at the birth of Buddha?

He was born.

What is a theist?

Someone who really likes the word "the".

What is meant by paradise or heaven?

You need a paradise to play a lot of games, like Monopoly.

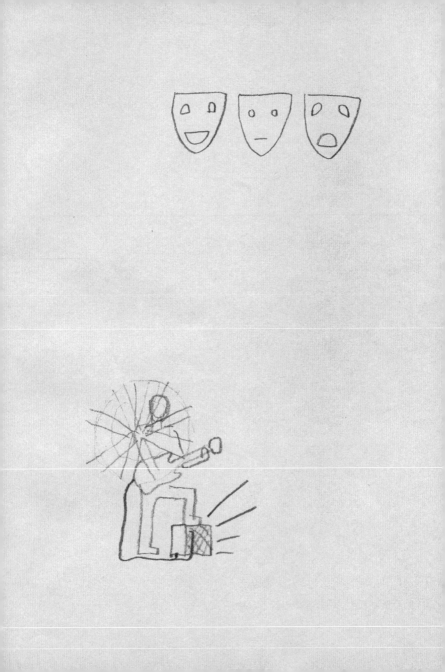

Subject: Drama and Music

In *King Lear*, what theme is most present when Edmund says, "The wheel is come full circle."?

CAR MAINTENANCE

Write about the character in *Romeo and Juliet* for whom you have the most sympathy.

I HAVE MOST SYMPATHY FOR THE AUDIENCE.

What advice would you give an actor playing Romeo?

It's just a teenage crush —
you'll get over it

Summarize Hamlet's famous soliloquy.

he didn't know what
pencil to use — 2B or not 2B

In *The Tempest*, why does Ariel sing to Gonzalo's ear?

SHE'S A MERMAID AND WANTS
   TO BE HUMAN.

Who do you consider to be the best teacher in *The History Boys*? Give reasons for your answer.

The history teacher because
      it's named after him!

What is meant by the terms "protagonist" and "antagonist"?

A PROTAGONIST IS FOR AGONISTS
AND AN ANTAGONIST IS AGAINST THEM

What are the components of a diminished seventh chord?

Fewer than the components of a whole seventh chord.

What is a fugue?

Someone who is on the run from the police.

What do you understand by the terms "homophonic" and "polyphonic?"

One doesn't like gay people and the other doesn't like parrots.

To which family of instruments does the clarinet belong?

clarinets are part of the wind-producing family

What is the time signature of this extract?

Time

What is an operetta?

The person at the switchboard who works the phones.

A high level of dissonance is often found in what type of music?

The kind that hurts people's ears.

In music, if "f" stands for "forte" what does "ff" stand for?

Eighty

Commonly found in jazz, what are blue notes?

Really sad, short letters.

UR
CAT'S
DEAD

What does it mean if a note has an accent?

It's written in another language.

The tempo of a piece of music tells you the underlying speed, what does the pulse tell you?

That it's alive

In music, what does andante mean?

How well the pasta is cooked

History and Classical Studies

Subject: ....

What is the Revolution of 1668 also sometimes known as?

The Goriest Revolution.

Who were the Bolsheviks?

A Russian ballet company

Who was the last tsar of Russia?

Tsar Nicholas the Last.

Explain the reasons for the Wall Street Crash of 1929.

Too many cars on the road, and bad drivers.

Who was Malcolm X?

The great-great-great-great-great-great-great grandson of Malcolm I.

Describe how Hitler took over Austria in 1938.

Quite quickly.

What else might you expect to find inside an
Egyptian pyramid, other than mummies?

Daddies

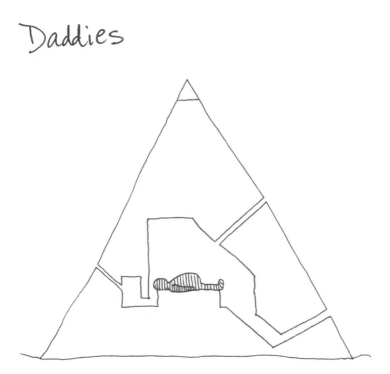

Explain the reason for the erection of the Berlin Wall.

To hold up the Berlin Ceiling.

Explain the dangers of life as a cowboy in the American Midwest.

High risk of being shot by Clint Eastwood.

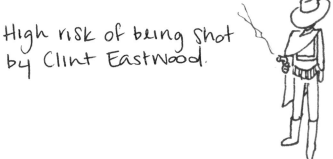

How was the Black Death dealt with?

By dying, usually.

Who were the Mountain Men, and why were they important?

Characters in Game of Thrones — very violent.

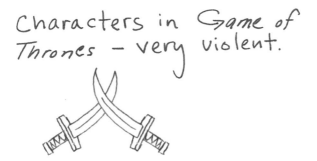

What was the Treaty of Versailles? Who signed it?

King Louis the
Something

Which of Henry VIII's wives was never imprisoned in the Tower of London?

Anne of Keys

Define capital punishment.

When you get in trouble for not putting a capital letter at the start of a sentence.

When Queen Elizabeth I came to the throne, what was the first thing she did?

Sat down.

Why did the infamous 1605 Gunpowder Plot fail?

Someone forgot to bring the matches.

What is the common translation for the famous phrase *carpe diem*?

Catch of the day.

How did the introduction of the "spinning mule" affect manufacturing in Great Britain during the Industrial Revolution?

There were more dancing donkeys to keep people happy.

Why did the Romans steal the Sabine women?

because they didn't know better

Who or what was a Cyclops?

The sound of a horse
riding a bike.

Who or what was Pegasus?

Pegasus are what my mom uses to hang out the laundry.

What monsters appear in the *Odyssey*?

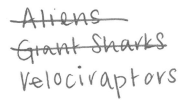

~~Aliens~~
~~Grant Sharks~~
Velociraptors

Why would you require a strong voice to perform in a Greek tragedy?

BECAUSE YOU'D HAVE TO SPEAK UP OVER ALL THE CRYING IN THE AUDIENCE.

The Romans came from which modern country?

ROMANIA.

The ancient Romans didn't have calculators, what did they use instead?

Their fingers.

Who were the Argonauts?

They were people sent up to the moon in the 1960s.

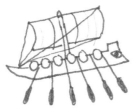

What didn't Roman children enjoy about education?

The same things I don't enjoy, such as exams like <u>this one</u>

Describe a Roman dinner party. How is it different from a modern dinner party?

There were MORE Romans there

Who was permitted to wear a toga?

People going to parties.

What was Roman life like for women?

the same as it was for men,
because they all wore dresses

Name one living person who visited the underworld.

Kate Beckinsale.

What is a fresco?

a type of coffee - with foam on top

Which civilisation established the first known use of democracy?

The Ancient Greeks.

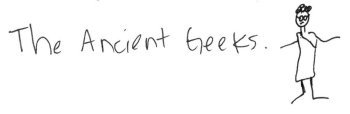

Describe public health in the nineteenth century.

a bit like public health in the twentieth century, just older

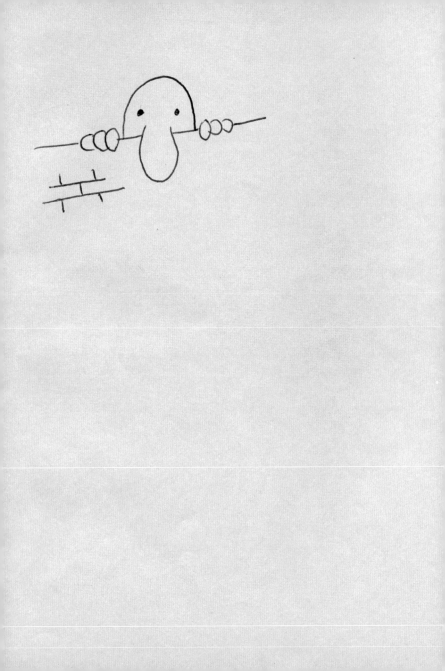

Media and Business Studies

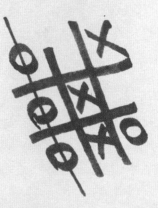

What does "self-regulation" mean in the context of media industries?

Deciding not to watch a whole series in one go on Netflix.

Explain how a media star can promote themselves using the Internet.

Putting a naked selfie on Instagram is a good way.

Explain the importance of niche markets to media industries.

They're where media people buy statues and other knick-knacks.

How can live streaming of reality shows cause legal problems for its producers?

If someone dies during the show, it suddenly turns into "Dead streaming" which is horrible for everyone.

What are the vital ingredients for a successful action film?

1. CAR CHASES
2. EXPLOSIONS
3. BRUCE WILLIS

Give a two-sentence pitch for your action film idea.

THERE ARE CAR CHASES AND EXPLOSIONS. THE LEAD ACTOR IS BRUCE WILLIS.

What does APR mean?

it's a short way of writing April

What is the security code on a credit card?

621 →

Jane has raised money at her school by selling cupcakes at lunchtimes. Give three other ways that she could raise money.

① put the money in stacks
② put it on shelves
③ hold it up high

What does "fair trade" mean?

when you swap your best comic for a really rare action figure

How does "fair trade" benefit others?

It stops people getting beaten up in
the playground.

What is meant by "brainstorming?"

It's a kind of really bad
headache.

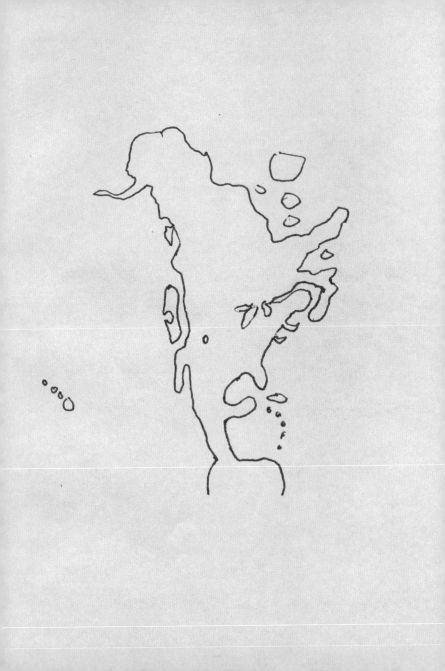

Subject: ....Geography........................

Name a characteristic of igneous rock.

IT'S VERY CLEVER

How are deserts formed?

MY FAVORITE WAY IS TO COMBINE
ICE CREAM, SLICED BANANAS, CARAMEL
SAUCE, & LOTS OF WHIPPED CREAM.

Give three examples of extreme weather.

1. weather for bungee jumping
2. weather for skydiving
3. weather for free climbing

How may a quarry be used for tourism purposes?

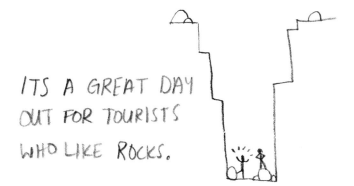

ITS A GREAT DAY
OUT FOR TOURISTS
WHO LIKE ROCKS.

Explain how heavy snow can cause disruption to daily life.

People get distracted from their work by snowball fights.

How do reservoirs and dams create a reliable water supply?

then write reminder notes to each other to make sure the supply is always reliable

Describe the different phase of the rock cycle.

It developed from Rhythm and Blues
and Jazz into Rock'n'Roll and
then into ⊒ℝ◎ℂℝ⊒

What do we call the currents in the earth's magma?

I don't know but I always spit
them out. I hate currents.

What is the name for professionals who monitor
and predict volcanic eruptions?

Vulcans.

Vulcans.

How can you tell where a river is on an Ordnance
Survey Map?

it's the part that's wet

Photos of the Alps show that glaciers have retreated over the last 50 years. One reason for this could be climate change. What could another reason be?

They're quite shy

What causes heavy rain?

too much fast food

What kind of wildlife would you expect to see in Antarctica?

Ants.

Name an expanse of salty water that's smaller than an ocean.

What is a continental plate?

moussaka

If a coastal arch collapses, what word would describe the remaining rock?

Lonely.

Turkey has seen a fall in its levels of export trade. Give one possible reason for this.

A rise in vegetarianism — fewer Turkeys being eaten.

The island of Madagascar houses many species that are not found anywhere else on the planet. Give one possible explanation for this.

Why would they move? Madagascar is awesome!

What is the name for the long lakes found at the bottom of deep glacial valleys?

Harry and Clive.

What does it mean if a waterfall has an overhang?

NOT ENOUGH EXERCISE, TOO MANY FRENCH FRIES!

TOOTH
HURTY

Subject: _Extra Credit_ ....

Explain how an ultrasound machine works.

By looking at tiny babies and drawing really bad pictures of them.

Give reasons why exercise helps a person lose weight.

they are so busy exercising they have no time to eat cake

Explain the health benefits of being outdoors.

You can fart and people might not notice.

What information should you have on a CV?

MOSTLY LIES, BUT ONLY IF YOU'RE SURE THEY WON'T BE FOUND OUT.

What is the most powerful light source known to man?

Why do we put salt on the roads when it snows?

to make them taste better

On a nature walk, where will you find humus?

IF YOU GO PAST A SUPERMARKET,
IT'S IN THE REFRIGERATED
SECTION BY THE COLESLAW

What are minerals?

Rules that are less important than major rules.

What are the characteristics of permeable rock?

it has curly hair

What do you make if you're a milliner?

less money than
a billiner.

Throwing is one method used to make pottery.
Name another.

Catching

What kinds of artists use collage?

THE KIND WHO PASS ALL
THEIR EXAMS AT SCHOOL

Name three benefits of regular training.

1. it's cheaper than driving
2. You can read on the train
3. they have a snack cart

How do you identify athlete's foot?

It's on the end of
athlete's leg

Why might a professional athlete take beta blockers?

If their current blockers aren't very
good and they want beta ones

How many different strokes do Olympic swimmers do in the Individual Medley?

It depends on how many cats are by the pool

Why do basketball players dribble close to the ground?

To reduce the chance of getting drool on their shorts

Assignment: Create a useful questionnaire to gauge your class's opinion.

1) How much do you enjoy this lesson?

☐ more than P.E.
☐ less than P.E.
☐ I didn't realize we were
    supposed to enjoy it

2) What's your favorite subject?

☐ lunch
☐ the one where we use clay
☐ this one of course. What's
    this one?

3) What do you think about homework?

☐ I don't think about it
☐ unnecessary torture
☐ all of the above